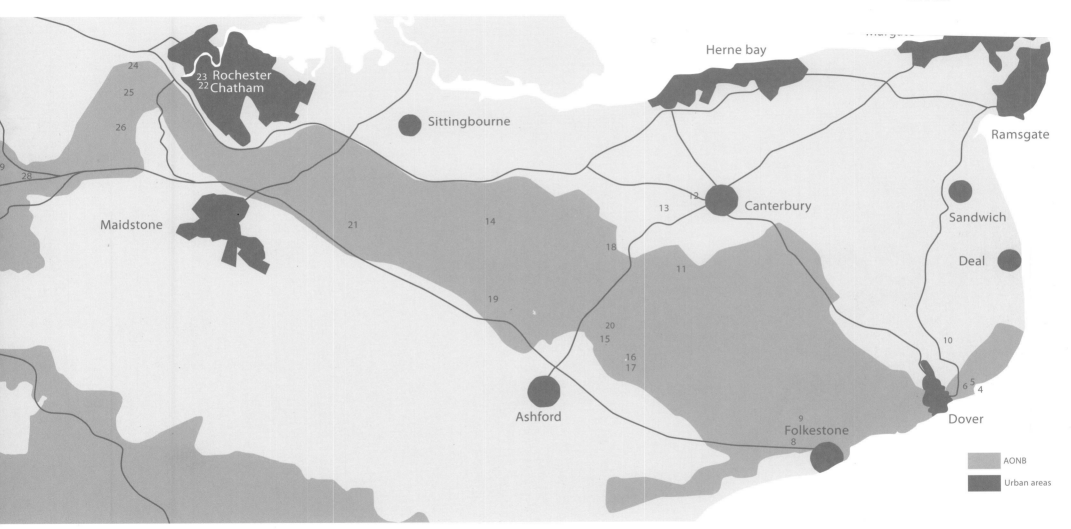

Herne bay

Margate

Ramsgate

24

25

26

23 Rochester
22 Chatham

Sittingbourne

Sandwich

9

28

Maidstone

21

14

12

13

Canterbury

18

11

Deal

19

20
15

16
17

10

Ashford

6 5
4

9
8

Folkestone

Dover

AONB

Urban areas

NORTH DOWNS
LANDSCAPES

*Exploring the Glorious English Countryside
on London's Doorstep*

Doug Kennedy

WIND*gather*
P R E S S

Windgather Press is an imprint of Oxbow Books

Published in the United Kingdom in 2015 by
OXBOW BOOKS
10 Hythe Bridge Street, Oxford OX1 2EW

and in the United States by
OXBOW BOOKS
908 Darby Road, Havertown, PA 19083

Hardback Edition: ISBN 978-1-909686-58-8
Digital Edition: ISBN 978-1-909686-59-5

A CIP record for this book is available from the British Library

Printed by Printworks Global Ltd. London & Hong Kong

For a complete list of Windgather titles, please contact:

UNITED KINGDOM
Oxbow Books
Telephone (01865) 241249
Fax (01865) 794449
Email: oxbow@oxbowbooks.com
www.oxbowbooks.com

UNITED STATES OF AMERICA
Oxbow Books
Telephone (800) 791-9354
Fax (610) 853-9146
Email: queries@casemateacademic.com
www.casemateacademic.com/oxbow

Oxbow Books is part of the Casemate Group

All photographs have been taken by Doug Kennedy (www.doug-kennedy.com)
apart from that on page 93, which is by Tom Stevens.

Title page: The Pilgrim's Way near Reigate

Flower meadow Medway Valley

Meadow on White Downs

On Hackhurst Downs

The duck pond at Otford

Footpath below Ranmore

Abinger Common stocks

INTRODUCTION

The North Downs are a range of hills that run east–west from the south-east tip of England, at Dover, to Farnham in Surrey. They skirt the southern edge of London, so for a long time have offered Londoners beautiful countryside to escape to for day trips, or for a home to commute to work from. A hundred years ago they were still quite remote, but London has grown, spreading onto Downland, and rail and road links have ensured that the many towns across the hills have also grown substantially in size. Indeed, the fight continues today to protect what is left of the Downs landscape from further development as population and land prices increase.

That being said, there is still a lot of unspoilt landscape, from farmland, to deep woods, to open grassland ridges with fantastic views across the Weald of Surrey and Kent; and it is these places that are the focus of this book. We go on a journey from the White Cliffs of Dover, through the rolling Kentish farm land with its open vistas and small villages, across the River Medway at Rochester, with its castle and cathedral, on to the wooded ridges past Sevenoaks, skirting the suburbs, into Surrey and across the River Mole to explore Leith Hill, then to Guildford and the River Wey, and over the Hog's Back to Farnham.

The geology of the Downs is important, as it defines the character of the landscape and dictates the way that it is used. The Downs are comprised largely of the same chalk formation that is the bedrock of the South Downs and other southern English hills. The chalk that underlies some of the greatest wine growing regions in France, including Champagne, is another part of the same formation. Globally this is an extremely rare rock and the landscape of the Downs is essentially, and uniquely, English, which makes it particularly precious.

The south-facing chalk ridge that forms the most distinct feature of the North Downs runs the full distance, broken only by the deep river valleys of the Wey, Mole, Darent, Medway and Stour, upon which many of the old downland towns are sited. The high points of the ridge are mostly overlaid with clay and flints, which makes the land very difficult to farm. This explains why they are heavily wooded, mostly with oak, beech and ash, and why many buildings are dressed with plough-wrecking flints. Below the ridge is a strip of 'greensand', a type of sandstone, which merges into sand and gravel deposits that form the 'Surrey Heath' landscape of bracken, heather and coniferous trees in the west.

This book attempts to capture the essence of the North Downs landscapes through carefully selected images that portray the main characteristics of each area. Inevitably, only a handful of settlements are included and many wonderful vistas have been left out, but I hope that the character and atmosphere shines through and brings you the pleasures of reminiscence and discovery.

This is a unique landscape that offers space, beauty and recreation to the population in the part of the country that is most under pressure from urban development, and it does need to be protected. The main organisations that provide this protection are listed at the end of this book.

The great historical geographer W. G. Hoskins said that the British landscape was the result of man rather than nature as we have been changing our environment since the introduction of agriculture in post Ice-age Britain. Once an enormous forest, the rolling hills of Surrey offer a domesticated charm of coppiced woods and patchwork-quilted fields nicely trimmed with hedges; it is a landscape we can feel comfortable with, as it wraps us in a rural dream of rose-covered cottages and flower-strewn meadows.

The White Cliffs of Dover

For many people leaving England, the White Cliffs are the last image of Britain that they see as they sail away, and the first for those approaching the country. They give Britain its earliest name, which is 'Albion' from the Greek for white. The English Channel is at its narrowest here, but the seas are fraught with dangerous currents, and these 90 metre (300 foot) cliffs form a solid defence against invasion.

Here you see the North Downs bedrock exposed: a solid block of chalk created by the shells of countless tiny plankton being deposited in a sea around a hundred million years ago. The chalk is at its broadest in Kent and the landscape is often rolling and open rather than hilly, with wide skies, and rather unlike the Downs further west where they are broken more by woods and valleys and the scale is smaller. This land was once covered in forest, but much of it was cleared for human settlement or to build ships, starting as long as 5000 years ago, and it is now mostly agricultural.

Chalk has its uses but, unlike limestone, it is not good for building as it is too soft and is eroded by rain water, which is why you do not see lots of white chalk-built houses. Instead, the clay that covers much of the surface of the Downs makes good bricks when baked, which became the norm for buildings throughout much of England.

Where the cliff dips, settlements have been established, and Dover became a major port, and the 'gateway' to England. This is because of its proximity to France and not because it forms a natural harbour. In fact, one can imagine that before large breakwaters were built, landing there from a boat must have been quite adventurous. Dover's strategically important position meant that it developed both as a port and a defensive site, and now the castle sits in a lofty position that dominates the town and harbour, able to watch the many ships entering and leaving the port.

Just along the coast, at the extreme south-east tip is the holiday village of St Margaret's-at-Cliffe. It sits atop the cliff with great views over the Channel to France, and a steep road with hairpin bends leads down to the bay, whose shingle beach is a pleasant sun trap, and also the normal start for cross-channel swimmers.

Left: The White Cliffs of Dover with St Margaret's-at-Cliffe in the middle, and Dover Harbour in the background

Right: The sea front at St Margaret's Bay

Dover Castle and the Start of the Downs

Dover Castle, which dominates the port, was first built in the 12th century by Henry II on previous fortifications, and has become known as 'The Key To England'. It has survived in better condition than most English castles because it was surrendered without a fight to the Parliamentarians during the Civil War in 1642. The fortifications were added to during the Napoleonic wars, and in the 20th century, extensive tunnels were dug to protect troops and secret wartime facilities including a command centre. In the image on the left, you can also see the Anglo-Saxon church of St Mary in Castro and the Roman lighthouse that became it's bell-tower. Today the site is owned by English Heritage and managed as a scheduled monument with tourism as its focus.

Chalk Grassland

This picture was taken from the National Trust land just to the south and illustrates the contrast between the original woodland that blanketed this countryside before humans started clearing it, and the chalk grassland that is maintained by grazing and clearing. The soil of chalk grassland tends to be quite shallow and poor in nutrients, but can be incredibly rich in plant species. Many, such as thyme, marjoram, rockrose, knapweed and trefoil have nectar-rich flowers that are much loved by butterflies. Thus, on a summer's day, you will see chalkhill and common blues, marbled whites, meadow browns, fritillaries and many more fluttering between the colourful flower heads. This rich ecosystem of miniatures is uniquely British but has become rare, and is still very much threatened by development owing mostly to an increasing human population in limited space, particularly in the south-east of England. Nowadays, the best is usually protected, either by the National Trust, local wildlife trusts, or by Natural England through legal protection as a Site of Special Scientific Interest, or National Nature Reserve.

Early Human Settlement

East Kent has been inhabited by humans since the last Ice Age and there is evidence of tree clearing and settlement as long as 5,000 years ago when the gentle nature of the climate and landscape helped early agriculture to prosper. The flints that litter the surface are very hard and sharp-edged when broken, so make excellent tools which are the epitome of the 'stone age'. Although the White Cliffs failed to keep out the Romans, Saxons and Normans (who entered at Hastings and took Dover from the land) benign conditions ensured that by the Middle Ages, the area became among the wealthiest in England.

Left: Dover Castle on its Down
Right, from top: Two Marbled White butterflies; Chalkhill Blue butterfly on knapweed; Silver-washed Fritillary on marjoram

The Folkestone Downs

From Maidstone, the route of the busy transport corridor to Dover that contains the M20 and A20 roads and the Eurostar and Dover mainline railways follows the foot of the North Downs. At Folkestone, this is joined by the huge Channel Tunnel rail terminal, sandwiched between the town and the steep 150 metre Downs scarp, spoiling what had been a very lovely piece of countryside. But as you head north from the concrete and noise and start to climb the steep hill, the contrast is dramatic, as you are suddenly presented with a range of beautiful hills covered in species-rich grassland.

The image above is taken from Stone Farm on the A20, which is where all the roads and railways come together in a noisy, rushing clump. However, following the footpaths will take you from here on a charming and peaceful walk into the Downs, where the views across the channel to the south and Romney Marsh to the west are hard to beat.

The hill on the right-hand side of this image is Summerhouse Hill that is a 148 metre out-rider of the main range. Its name derives from a gazebo which was built on the summit of the hill by landowners prior to the land being taken over by the Ministry of Defence for army training. The gazebo does not survive having been burnt down during enthusiastic Guy Fawkes night celebrations in 1935.

Much of the Downs land around Folkestone is owned by Eurotunnel, with some residual army training areas, but the land is now managed by The White Cliffs Countryside Partnership. This was set up to "help conserve and enhance the special coast and countryside of Dover and Shepway districts, and make it accessible to all." (http://www.whitecliffscountryside. org.uk/) and includes local councils, Eurotunnel, English Nature, wildlife trusts and other stake-holders.

Roaming a Vibrant Downs Landscape

Folkestone Downs is one of the largest areas of unimproved chalk downland in Kent, but this takes management if it is not to return to scrub. The grass has to be grazed to keep it short, and as sheep can graze too close to the ground for the native wildflowers to survive, cattle are used which allow for a longer ground vegetation. There used to be many rabbits, but numbers have diminished owing largely to myxamatosis."

The extensive flora includes Horseshoe Vetch and Small Scabious, as well as scarce species such as Bedstraw Broomrape along with many species of orchid (see page 27). Up to 32 species of butterfly have been recorded along with many moths and birds.

The image on the right is near the top of Tolsford Hill, (which has a large communications tower on its 181 metre summit) and shows the lie of the land, with a mixture of rough grass, gorse, blackthorn and other scrub plants, and woodland. You can see the main body of the Downs in the distance, with a deep valley between.

The stile is on the North Downs Way at its most south-westerly point. As well as ramblers and dog walkers, many cyclists enjoy these hills, and very close to here is a steep byway that is used by four-wheel-drive enthusiasts.

Overleaf Left: The rolling agricultural landscape of East Kent
Overleaf Right: Chartham Downs

Agricultural Icons of the East Kent Downs

From the first human settlements in Kent it has been a land where people have prospered, and that is because things grow well there, be it grain, vegetables, fruit or livestock, earning it the occasional title of 'The Garden of England'. Which crops have been grown over the years has depended upon the soil type, which varies from very fertile to nearly unusable at the flinty crest of the Downs, but also upon the demand, which for centuries has centred on London. Many landowners have become well off, the wealthiest of all possibly being the Archbishopric of Canterbury which has owned a great many manors across Kent, and thus managed much of the land. The manor houses were usually built right next to the church, a custom that has determined the character of many English villages. Kentish farmers have also been innovative in agriculture in their quest for greater productivity, for instance in developing crop rotation, using leguminous plants to replenish soil nutrients.

Kent has a long association with the cultivation of orchard fruit, in particular apples, and also for hops for the brewing industry. This trend was very strong during the 19th century when Charles Dickens wrote in *The Pickwick Papers*, "Kent, sir – everybody knows Kent – apples, cherries, hops and women". As well as being profitable, these crops had a social impact because they gave East Londoners the opportunity of an annual working holiday in the fresh air picking the hop flowers and apples: the conditions tended to be very basic, but people seemed usually to enjoy the experience and earn some cash on the way.

These crops have also had a strong impact on the landscape, with thousands of acres of blossom in the spring, and the building of oast houses, which remain an iconic feature and have been retained by many farms, but as use for housing or storage rather than roasting hops. Their purpose was to dry the hop flowers which give beer its character and bitterness, acting a bit like a tumble dryer. A fire at the base of the oast heated the hops above it and dried them as the cowl on top allowed air to circulate and moisture to escape. Hop growing declined towards the end of the 20th century owing to a move to lagers, and overseas competition, whilst East Enders became better off and wanted actual holidays! Few hops are grown in Kent now, although English ale is a resurgent industry.

Apple orchards were also grubbed out because they became uneconomic as overseas competition from more consistent, saleable fruit meant that English apples began to disappear. Fortunately, a vigorous campaign for people to recognise the value of their home grown fruit has resulted in a lot of orchards being replanted, using varieties that suit the modern taste.

Left: Oast houses and apple boxes at a farm near Canterbury
Right: Apple orchard at Chartham Hatch

Eastling: an old Downs village

Eastling is a small rural village situated high on the Downs, about four miles from Faversham. This is one of the areas where the land was once only suitable for sheep or forestry because of the shallow, flinty soil, but with advances in agriculture combined with a lot of work, it can be made to produce a lot more. Until recent times, the farms grew mostly cherries and flowers, however nothing stays still, and the village website makes interesting reading about the history of the surrounding agriculture which supports its residents. It says:

> "The village is surrounded by agricultural land, much of it part of the Belmont Estate. The current depressed agricultural economy has brought an increase in arable lands, while the area's traditional horticulture has declined.
>
> The broad agricultural economy is in a period of transition, reflected locally. The financial underpinning is shifting away from food production quotas towards the land. Government-sponsored rural programmes now emphasise attractive landscape, and protection of the natural habitat for flora and fauna." (www.eastling.co)

The village has a pub and a school and a couple of fine manor houses, plus St Mary's Church. This has Saxon origins, but the current building was started in the 11th century and added to in stages up to recent times. The yew tree on the left of the tower is regarded as ancient, and may be 2,000 years old.

Wye: ancient routes

Wye is a substantial village which grew from being an important crossing point of the River Great Stour, originally a ford on the route from Canterbury to Hastings, but also on the Pilgrim's Way. Because of this, the church and town have an association with pilgrims and other travellers going back over two millennia.

In 1447, Wye College was founded by John Kempe, a native of Wye who became Archbishop of Canterbury and Lord Chancellor. It was originally a Latin school and seminary, but became a famous agricultural college, and has been part of London University since 1900.

John Kemp also refurbished and added to the Church of St Gregory and St Martin from whose churchyard the image on the right of the elegant High Street is taken.

Left: St Mary's Church, Eastling
Right: Wye High Street from the churchyard

The North Downs Scarp

Possibly the most outstanding characteristic of the North Downs is the steep scarp slope that runs for most of the 150 mile length of the Downs on the south southern side. It is up to 200 metres high and in the Kentish east, snakes roughly north-west from the coast behind Folkestone, past Stowting and on to Wye on the River Great Stour. Just before Wye there is a particularly steep section known as the Devil's Kneading Trough, which is a spectacular coomb cut by landslides as the last ice-age retreated and the land thawed. It is now part of the Wye National Nature Reserve in which the chalk grassland is renowned for containing 21 species of orchid, including the lady orchid, fly orchid, the rare early spider orchid and the man orchid.

The area is managed to create an ideal habitat for many vertebrate, insect and flower species, many of which are unique to chalk grasslands. In order that scrub doesn't take over, the area is grazed by cattle whose browsing keeps the vegetation low.

The image on the right is taken from immediately above the Trough, looking out over the Weald of Kent and Romney Marsh. On a clear day, you can also see the English Channel from this point.

The Pilgrim's Way and the North Downs Way

There is an ancient trackway running from Folkestone to Stonehenge that has been in use since prehistoric times, 5,000 years ago. From the Middle Ages, it was used as a route for pilgrims to travel from Winchester to Canterbury, and the section that follows the North Downs scarp is now called the Pilgrim's Way. It is the location of Chaucer's Canterbury Tales and it remains an established route to this day, mostly footpath although some sections are drivable.

The North Downs Way is a long-distance footpath route that runs alongside, or coincides with the Pilgrim's Way, from Farnham in Surrey to the River Stour in Kent. Here it divides and does a loop to Canterbury then along the north side of the Downs to Dover and back along the south ridge to Wye and across the Stour making its total length 153 miles (246 Km).

Chilham Castle (*left*)

The great house pictured here has replaced a stone keep and fortification that was built in the 1170s by Fulbert de Dover in a prominent position overlooking the River Great Stour as a stronghold inland from Dover Castle. In 1216, the castle was occupied briefly by the Dauphin, the heir to the French throne, who was trying to usurp King John with the support of many of the barons. He had captured Canterbury, but got no further as King John died and the barons decided to enthrone the infant Henry II instead.

Subsequently, the castle fell into ruin and was largely dismantled, and the current house was built by Sir Dudley Digges in 1616. It is built in the Italian Renaissance style and on a very unusual hexagonal pattern. The property has changed hands many times, and today it remains privately owned.

Chilham Village is a pretty place with a charming village square, whose appearance, like many otherwise lovely villages, is often spoiled by parked cars. But it has many picturesque houses of great antiquity and has been a location for a number of films, including the 1944 film *A Canterbury Tale*, *The Amorous Adventures of Moll Flanders* and BBC's 2009 adaptation of Jane Austen's novel *Emma*.

The Archbishop's Palace, Charing

An Archbishop's palace was built here in 1348 as a place to stay when the prelate was travelling between London and Canterbury. This was one of a string of medieval palaces for the purpose, located at Charing, Otford and Croydon, which will have witnessed many historic events as bishops, lords and commoners will have visited the Head of the English Church to discuss important affairs of the day, and it is known that Henry VII and VIII stayed at the palace. However in 1545 Henry VIII seized the palaces for the Crown as part of the Dissolution and they were sold off, and this one has been in private hands ever since. Now only parts of Charing Palace remain, including the front wall and gate pictured on the right, but these give the approach to St Peter and St Paul Church a feeling of stepping back in time. What's left of the palace itself is now a rather extraordinary farm house and barn; a piece of living history.

Charing village also has great charm, with a long, picturesque high street and, like Wye, is situated on the Pilgrims' Way only one day's walk from Canterbury.

Left: Chilham Castle
Right: Charing Palace gateway

The Valley of the Great Stour

The source of the River Great Stour is in a 'greensand' ridge south of Ashford, and only a few miles from the English Channel. Greensand is a type of sandstone that runs along the south side of the chalk that forms the Downs, occasionally rising as ranges of hills that sometimes merge into the North Downs, particularly in West Surrey south of Dorking. Two Stour tributaries flow northwards to meet at Ashford, then on to Wye and through a gap in the North Downs that narrows, before the valley opens right out at Canterbury into a flat landscape of reclaimed marshes. The river empties into the North Sea close to a village called Cliff's End, an accurate descriptive as this is the northerly limit of the coastal white cliffs comprised of North Downs chalk.

The image on the left shows the gentle landscape of the Great Stour Valley near Wye with the Downs rising on the far side to the west. The Pilgrim's Way (and North Downs Way) traces the bottom of the slope in the final section before Canterbury, following the Great Stour through its gap in the Downs. As travel-weary Canterbury pilgrims passed Chartham, one can imagine that they would have felt a great upsurge of joy and anticipation so close to the end of their journey, and the inspiring sight of the towers of Canterbury Cathedral must have been wondrous indeed!

Until the 1970s, the land through the gap was used to grow hops, but now huge apple, pear and plum orchards cover most of the valley from one side to the other (see pages 12–13).

Left: The Great Stour Valley near Wye
Above: Arable farming near Hollingbourne

Rochester Town

Along their length, the North Downs are interrupted by deep river valleys, the first of which is the Great Stour at Canterbury, and the second is the River Medway at Rochester. The Medway is a much greater river and strategically more important, being close to where it joins the Thames Estuary at Sheerness. The Diocese of Rochester, based at the lovely Norman Rochester Cathedral, is the second oldest in England. The town also has strong naval links, particularly for ship building, and is now merged with Chatham, the old home of the Royal Navy Dockyards. That merger, and subsequent administrative changes to borough boundaries resulted in it losing its city status and it became one of the Medway towns along with Gillingham and Chatham. However a movement to reinstate its city status continues to this day.

Apart from the castle and cathedral, there are many historic buildings in Rochester, and walking down the High Street you can feel you are walking through history. Charles Dickens was an admirer and lived nearby at Gads Hill Place, Higham. He based many of his novels in the area, including *The Pickwick Papers*, *Great Expectations* and *The Mystery of Edwin Drood*.

Rochester Castle

The Bishops of Rochester have been very powerful, and in the 12th century, the future King William II got Bishop Gundulf to build Rochester Castle, which has one of the best preserved keeps in England. The castle was put under siege several times up to the 15th century during internal power struggles but like most English castles has never had to defend against foreign invaders. It sits on the river edge of the town in a commanding position, perched high on a cliff with long views up and down the Medway Valley.

Cultural Note:
On crossing the Medway, we are passing from East Kent to West Kent, and there are differences. During the Dark Ages, they may have been settled by different invading groups: Jutes to the east, and Saxons to the west, but since time immemorial, if you are from East Kent, you are a Man or Maid of Kent, and if from West Kent, you are a Kentish Man or Maid.

Left: Rochester High Street
Right: Rochester Castle

Overleaf Left: Flower-filled meadow on the North Downs Way above Cuxton
Overleaf Right: The hamlet of Upper Bush

Difficult Soil High Up in the Downs

The photographs on this page are both taken on the North Downs Way on the ridge above the River Medway within a kilometre of each other. They are fields that have been cut within the woods that farmers seem to have given up on as unproductive for agriculture, and the reason can be seen in the image below. The ground is covered in flints that, even when cleared, are endlessly replaced from below, and in addition, the shallow soil on top of the alkaline chalk makes some nutrients unavailable to many plants and tends not to hold water. This can be overcome with a lot of input of organic material and nutrients, but that is a big investment.

Many a farmer has broken his plough and his back on such land to no avail, and this is the reason that so much of the high downland is not farmed, but forested or else used for grazing sheep.

This poor soil, however, can support a huge variety of wild flowers that often grow in profusion, as can be seen on the left. The image shows clover (*Trifolium pratense*) at the base, oxeye daisies (*Chrysanthemum leucanthemum*) in the middle and common sowthistle (*Sonchus oleraceus*) at the top, which are all common weed species of agricultural land as well as being attractive wild flowers. These species need a more nutrient-rich soil than the wild flowers of unimproved chalk grassland, and without any input for several years will be replaced by scrub then forest as the nutrients leach away.

Orchids of the Chalk Grassland

From April to September, where chalky soil is undisturbed, many species of orchid can be found growing. Some are easy to find, such as the common spotted and pyramidal orchids, which can grow in large groups, occasionally covering large areas, whilst others are small and hard to spot, such as the ordinary-looking twayblade, with its small green flowers.

All British orchids are small compared to their tropical cousins, but they are mostly very pretty and all unusual, or downright weird, in their structure and habits, so are worth looking out for.

Top left: Pyramidal Orchid (*Anacamptis pyramidalis*)
Top right: Bee Orchid (*Ophrys apefera*)
Middle left: Greater Butterfly Orchid (*Platanthera chlorantha*)
Middle right: Early Purple Orchid (*Orchis mascula*)
Lower left: Common Spotted Orchid (*Dactylorhiza fuchsii*)
Lower right: Common Twayblade (*Neottia ovata*)
Below: Orchids spread across chalk grassland

The West Kent Landscape

Probably the most iconic man-made shape in Kent is the tapering roof and cowl of the oast houses. These remain common in West Kent, and in most cases have been turned into character dwellings and merged into the accompanying house. The structures on these pages are round, unlike those on page 12 whose square design is more recent.

Below the scarp of the Downs, the land becomes less hilly as it drops into the 'Low Weald', which is the valley between the North and South Downs where the soil is more fertile and easily worked than among the flinty chalk. The West Kent landscape tends to be smaller in scale than in East Kent, made up of a patchwork of fields, woods, towns and villages.

As you move west, closer to London, urban development and large roads cover increasing amounts of land, to the extent that the open landscape can almost be obliterated, as occurs between Caterham and Redhill in Surrey. However, even quite close to the City, there is still a lot of tranquillity to be found high in the Downs from where magnificent views open both to the south, over the Weald, and northwards to the London itself. A rambler on the North Downs Way in these parts, is treated to a varied and lovely landscape of deep woods interspersed with sudden fields or open grassland, often with horses grazing, and panoramas that open up unexpectedly.

It was not always thus, and in the days of Chaucer, pilgrims would have been travelling through great forests for days on end, seeing only trees and the odd clearing, only opening out where sheep were grazed. This changed most when a huge proportion of England's trees were felled to build ships and fuel furnaces during the 17th to 19th centuries, leaving a stark, scarred landscape that became available for landscaping, or building upon.

Left: A converted oast near Wrotham
Right: Looking south into the Weald near Wrotham

Overleaf Left: A successful crop on the Downs crest in the spring sunshine
Overleaf Right: Looking north-east to London Docklands from above Sevenoaks

Otford

Otford lies in the River Darent Valley, which flows through another gap in the Downs. The Pilgrim's Way descends steeply through the forest, and ramblers leave the tranquility of the high Downs and meet the A225 Sevenoaks road, entering the village by the train station. A hundred yards further on, you arrive at a charming green and pond which is a truly unique spot. The pond forms the centre of a roundabout, circled by the A road, and is the only such roundabout in the United Kingdom. In 2013 it was given the Best Roundabout Award (yes, there is one!) and it is now a listed structure.

Around the pond and accompanying green are arranged the church, a manor house and a quaint row of shops including a tea shop from which one can watch the ducks dabble and the traffic pass. The Church, dedicated to St Bartholemew, was started in the 11th century and it contains one of the few surviving early Norman naves. The sturdy tower is 12th century and was crowned with its spire at a later date.

Otford also possesses the remains of another Archbishop's palace, though far less well preserved than is the case in Charing. This would probably have been the next stop on the Archbishop's route to London after Rochester. Archaeological remains suggest that Otford may have adopted Christianity at a very early point, during Roman times.

Left: St Bartholemew's Church, Otford

Right: 'Pickmoss', a restored 14th-century house

The Kent–Surrey Border

As you approach the county border, the land begins to come under a lot of pressure from housing and roads, in fact the borders of Surrey, Kent and Greater London meet between Biggin Hill (G. London) and Westerham (Kent), a couple of kilometres from the image on this page. The first major sign of urban encroachment is where the M25 crosses the Downs on the western side of the River Darent, descending into the valley a couple of miles west of Otford and is joined by the M26 on its way west towards Redhill. Then the tentacles of London, their sinews marked out in railways and big roads, stretch out at Biggin Hill, Warlingham, Caterham and Tadworth, whilst the green spaces between become gradually encircled.

In spite of this, you can find peace even in the pressured Kent/Surrey border area and, along the crest of the Downs, the views are still amazing. On the left, the North Downs Way has climbed the steep scarp and is about to plunge into a bit of woodland. The trees are decked in their early summer foliage, and here the route passes between two oak trees before entering the woodland under a copper beech. Beech and oak are the most typical trees of the chalk downs, although copper beeches are unusual. As you walk here in the summer, wildflowers are dotted among the grass and sometimes form colourful clumps where butterflies dance.

The photograph on the right is taken from the Pilgrim's Way about a mile inside the actual Surrey county line and is looking east, back into Kent, across the fields of grain sloping down to the Weald. The white building nestled in the wood is called Pilgrim House, and there is also a Pilgrim's Farm a little further to the west.

Left: Heading west on the Pilgrim's Way close to the Surrey border

Right: Looking east along the descending Downs slope from the Surrey side of the county border

Motorways in the North Downs

Between Reigate/Redhill and Caterham in Surrey, the Downs almost disappear. At this point, the M25 is crossed by the M23 motorway that is heading south towards Gatwick Airport: this junction is shown in the aerial photograph, with the village of Merstham tucked between the two in the middle distance. The M25 was only constructed towards the end of the 20th century and has had a major impact on the landscape, cutting the heart out of forests and introducing noise and pollution to a previously tranquil and beautiful countryside. When planning new motorways, the priority is to minimise the destruction of built property, and because so much of the land is already developed, the obvious route is usually through areas that had previously been left alone because of their beauty. One extreme example of this lies a bit further west, where the A3/M25 junction was placed bang in the middle of Wisley common, previously one of the largest remaining ancient woods in Surrey. In the crowded south-east of England, governments don't seem to find it very difficult to sacrifice what countryside we have left on the altar of Development.

This is why organisations like the National Trust, Woodland Trust, Wildlife Trusts and the Royal Society for the Protection of Birds are so vital in the unending fight to conserve landscape and wildlfe. Details of these organisations are given at the end of this book.

Reigate and Redhill

In the Domesday Book, the area that Reigate sits on was listed as 'Cherchefelle', which probably means "open space by the hill", and the town didn't start to be formed until the 12th century. At this time, William de Warenne, the Earl of Surrey, had Reigate Castle built (it was largely dismantled five hundred years later). Reigate does indeed sit by a very steep hill that is Reigate Down, but it lies on a hard greensand which is quarried to make roofing tiles and known as 'Reigate stone'.

The town really began to develop when the Brighton Railway came nearby at what is now Redhill in 1841; indeed, it was the railway station that caused Redhill to form from smaller settlements in the area. The two towns together make a single conurbation served by two railway lines, one running north–south, and the other east–west making Redhilll station quite a major junction. It is also a next to the M25/M23 junction so is extraordinarily well served by transport links, whilst still being not too large and within pleasant countryside.

Left: Aerial photograph of the M25/M23 junction with Merstham in the middle right
Right: Reigate town from the Downs scarp

Protecting What We Love: the battle for Banstead Downs

Banstead Downs and Commons are areas between Sutton to the north, Walton-on-the-Hill to the west and the M25 to the south that remain largely open and comprised of woods and grassland. They are hugely popular with people from the surrounding towns for recreation, exercise and dog walking and also contain some important wildlife habitats.

Until the late 19th century, much of the land on the Downs was common land, that is, owned by the community with access and grazing rights. As London grew southwards and railways were built, some wealthy men saw an opportunity to take over, or buy up, the commons and build houses on them, and many were successful. However, in the Banstead area, the Commoners objected, and mounted a lengthy legal case which eventually resulted in an Act Of Parliament that protected the commons from development. They are now managed by the Banstead Commons Conservators who have a statutory duty to "ensure safe and free access of the public to the commons and to protect the commons from damage and trespass." The notice board to the right contains notices to the public placed by the Conservators.

This was a very important victory as Commoners in areas like Coulsdon, Godalming and Limpsfield followed their example and fought and won their own battles against developers to protect their commons.

The folk enjoying Sunday lunch in the open are outside the Sportsman pub on the southern side of Banstead Downs. This is a very popular spot on a sunny weekend when people from surrounding towns can walk a few miles, enjoying the lovely views, and knowing that a cool drink and some food can be enjoyed in happy company at the end of it.

Throughout the Downs, country and village pubs are a tremendously important feature, acting as a focus for motorists from the towns, and offering refreshment to walkers, horse riders and cyclists. Most of them have been there for hundreds of years and are often in interesting buildings, providing the unique atmosphere of the English pub. It isn't an easy business, as they are often very quiet during the week or when the weather is poor, and then have to cope with vast surges of people when it's nice. An English countryside without its pubs is virtually unthinkable, as they are etched on the national consciousness, but like any other business need to be used to survive.

Left: Sunday lunch at The Sportsman pub on Banstead Downs
Right: Banstead Common

Margery Wood: a fragmented habitat

Bluebells (*Hyacinthoides non-scripta*) are a springtime delight across much of the United Kingdom, but in the chalk down woodland they seem to do particularly well, forming deep blue-purple carpets across the forest floor. This is Margery Wood, which is a scrap of woodland, hemmed between the M25, houses and farmland. Before the motorway was built, it was larger and would have been a peaceful place from which you would emerge onto Colley Hill, with its brilliant views towards the South Downs. It is still a pleasant place and popular with walkers, but there is the constant buzz of motorway traffic in the background, and you have to cross a footbridge to get to the view now.

Fragmentation of woods and other habitats by roads and new settlements is a particular problem for wildlife, whose local populations become isolated, resulting in problems with breeding and feeding. It is also extremely perilous for animals to cross these new roads and road kills by fast-moving traffic are on the increase. The Woodland Trust does a great deal of work in finding ways to link habitats together, creating 'wildlife corridors' by buying land between woods, or getting landowners and managers to plant trees to link them.

The Woodland Trust also focuses on protecting ancient woods, which means land that has been continuously wooded for at least 600 years, because they contain the greatest biodiversity. Big carpets of bluebells are one indicator of an ancient wood, as are wood anenomes (*Anenome nemorosa*), seen in the image on the right among a carpet of primroses (*Primula vulgaris*).

Local people do a great deal of work to maintain and improve habitats, so on Banstead Downs, the Conservators and associated groups work hard to restore damaged land through weed, scrub or rabbit clearance, so that the rarer native plants can return.

Left: Bluebells in Margery Wood
Right: Primroses and wood anenomes

Overleaf Left: The view west from Reigate Hill, along the Downs scarp
Overleaf Right: The view west from the Buckland Hills

Reigate and Buckland Downs

The images on pages 42 and 43 are taken from the top of the Downs scarp, above Reigate, whilst that opposite is taken from below the Downs, looking towards Juniper Hill. The house at the top of the hill on the left is quite near to where the former photographs were taken.

The image on page 42 looks westward along the Downs scarp from Reigate Hill in which you can see the character of the landscape in this area. The woodland at the top of the hill is a mixture of beech, ash, yew and juniper that has a rather sudden border with the open chalk grassland. Such areas have normally been cleared to graze sheep, and as it is very nutrient poor, the turf tends to be of the type that is very rich in wildflowers, including orchids. Down in the valley, the land is mostly agricultural, but field sizes are moderate and interspersed with managed woodlands. In the distance, the next spur is Box Hill, and behind that is White Downs.

On page 43, the photograph is taken from a footpath above a private garden belonging to one of a row of houses built on the crest of the Buckland Hills above Reigate. It is a lovely spot to live, but it is also fortunate for the rest of us that such development was curtailed as we might well have been denied a lot of the panoramas on offer. In this spot, the footpath runs behind a 6 foot high fence for most of its length with no views at all.

The image opposite shows arable fields on Underhill Farm that illustrate the difficulty of farming this chalky, flinty soil with bare patches around the borders in spite of it having been a damp summer. The Downs slopes are forested, among which the darker green is yew trees.

Buckland
The image on this page is in the village of Buckland that lies below Buckland Down on the A25 half way between Reigate and Dorking. The green, with its pond, are shown here (the wooden building is not a church), photographed from by the main road, whilst on the opposite (south) side of the road are a pretty row of shops and the church.

The village has an amusing legend centred on a large boulder that used to exist in Shag Brook with a blood red vein of iron ore running through it. This was supposed to house a monstrous horse called the Buckland Shag that would eat passing travellers. However, in 1757, the local parson, Willoughby Bertie, had the stone removed from the brook and thrown from a cliff in Devon, ending the story that was probably told to amuse locals and scare strangers travelling through this wild region.

Left: A view across fields towards Juniper Hill
Right: Buckland village pond and green

Steep Ways and Wild Woods on the Scarp Slopes

The North Downs and Pilgrim's Ways coincide throughout this part of their journey, following the ancient track of the pilgrims. They mostly stick to the top of the ridge, but at times descend the steep scarp, plunging two hundred-odd feet before rising again a bit further on. The natural state of this land is dense forest, but it is interspersed with areas of chalk grassland where the trees have been cleared, usually to graze sheep. These woods often have a dense canopy along with a scrubby underbrush of holly, hawthorn, ivy and other forest floor plants that make it difficult to stray from the path. Then in some places, the chalk has been quarried, so you can encounter sudden cliffs that can be dangerous to the unwary. All this means that, visually, walking the Pilgrim's Way is full of variety, with long panoramic views one minute, and deep, dark forest the next before opening out onto a farm, or finding yourself on the edge of a village.

Some areas of this steep slope are covered in yew trees, creating a quite different atmosphere as other species are inhibited and only the yew grows on an otherwise empty forest floor. This is not because the yew is poisonous, which it is, but because it is a very dense evergreen that casts too deep a shade for underbrush to develop, and the canopy of the trees tends to merge into one. Yew trees take a long time to grow, and can be very ancient. They have long been associated with churchyards and it has been suggested that they were planted on the graves of plague victims to protect and purify the dead. Yew trees have been seen as symbols of immortality, but also seen as omens of doom.

Yew timber is rich orange-brown in colour, closely grained and incredibly strong and durable; it was used for making the English long bow which was known to be very powerful, but also very hard to bend. Although poisonous to humans, the fruit is eaten by birds such as the blackbird, mistle thrush, song thrush and fieldfare, and small mammals such as squirrels and dormice. The leaves are eaten by caterpillars of the satin beauty moth.

Left: The Pilgrims/North Downs Way descends the scarp near Reigate

Right: A yew wood on the scarp

Epsom and its Race Course

Epsom lies on the dip slope on the northern side of the North Downs, and was once a market and spa town surrounded by countryside. It is now on the outer edge of London suburbia, having linked up with Ewell and Sutton as land was filled in with housing. The town gave its name to Epsom Salts, from the time when the town's mineral spring baths were popular. In those days, the spring water was boiled down to produce a powder whose chemical name is magnesium sulphate, a compound which is still on sale for people to put into their bath water to ease their aching joints.

It is a busy commuter town with a fine high street and market place, and it has retained several commons and parks that provide lots of green space around it. However, Epsom is most famous for the Epsom Downs Racecourse that spreads across the hills close by, between Tattenham Corner (where there is a train station), Langley Vale and Tadworth. Horse racing has taken place there since the 17th century and two of the 'classic' events of the racing year, the Oaks and The Epsom Derby date back to when they were started for personal sport by the Earl of Derby and have continued ever since. These downs have a wonderful dry, open turf and the gentle undulations provide great racing and the elevated position offers gorgeous views in all directions. In earlier times, there was the added benefit that ladies who were not interested in the racing could 'take the waters' whilst the gentlemen went to the races, which would have been a most convenient arrangement.

The course has always been popular, and today, it is a very smart place with white rails tracing huge loops across the grassy sward, and white stands that are landmarks seen from many miles away. Alternatively, you can walk across the racecourse on public footpaths which gives a one a rather unique perspective on the Downs whilst watching the race horses gallop by.

Left: Epsom town centre on a winter market day
Right: Epsom Downs Racecourse on a race day

Dorking Town

Dorking lies in a particularly lovely location in the Vale of Holmesdale, between the chalk Downs and the greensand Surrey Hills. It is at the crossroads of ancient routes and probably started to develop as a staging post; in fact there is archaeological evidence of rest houses going back to the 12th century used by the Knights Templar. Nowadays, the town has several old pubs, some of which were coaching inns, including the White Horse and the Bull's Head.

It is at the junction of the A29 running north–south, which follows the Roman road of Stane Street, and the A25 which runs east–west along the valley, though it has been spared from the blight of motorways. These days, the Pilgrim's Way passes a kilometre to the north of the town, crossing the pretty River Mole at Burford Bridge, but that has not always been the case. Dorking's main church of St Martin is built on the original route at an ancient religious site.

Dorking is known as quite a wealthy town, and this was helped by the arrival of the railway in the 19th century. With its lovely location and excellent transport connections, it became a magnet for better-off people who worked in London, but wanted their families to be raised and weekends spent in the countryside. It is also a busy market town and has been a leisure destination, particularly for Londoners, since the 18th century.

Box Hill

Some might say that Box Hill is more famous than it should be: at the main viewing point, it is only 172 metres high, and from the north and east, it is simply another point on the main ridge. However, its west and south faces are very steep, so quite dramatic, and the views over the Mole Valley, Dorking and the Weald from Salomons Memorial are quite remarkable. Thousands of people visit it each year to enjoy the view and have a picnic, or visit the National Trust cafe situated there. The energetic can climb the footpath from Burford Bridge, which crosses a steep open grassy sward before passing through woodland that opens out at the main viewpoint. The cyclist in the image to the left has just reached this, having ridden up the zig-zag road, which includes the only hairpin bends in this part of the world.

The River Mole cuts through the North Downs right against Box Hill and has carved a vertiginous slope in the chalk which is covered in the box trees (*Buxus sempervirens*) that give the hill its name.

Left: A cyclist arrives at the main viewpoint on Box Hill

Right: The old pump surmounted by its route signpost to Horsham and Guildford at the busy intersection in the middle of town

The Mole Valley and Denbies Wine Estate

The beauty of the Mole Valley has made it a major attraction for visitors and also a desirable location to live in, to the extent that some very grand houses have been built there. Perched on a hill on the west side of the valley is Norbury Park House (seen above the winery in the image on this page) which was built by William Locke in the 18th century. One later occupant was Marie Stopes, the British scientist and writer, who lived there from 1938 to 1958. The wooded parkland that surrounds Norbury contains some of the most ancient yew trees in Surrey and is now mostly open to the public and very popular for walking and cycling.

On the east side of the valley, above Leatherhead, is Cherkley Court, which was built in 1893 and later owned by Lord Beaverbrook, the press baron and is still owned by his foundation. However at the time of writing, a major battle has been going on for some years concerning the estate's future as the owners want to turn it into a luxury hotel and golf course, which is being opposed by people who point to the number of golf courses already in the area, and who want to preserve the landscape.

A third mansion was Denbies, owned by the builder, Thomas Cubbitt. It fell into disrepair and was demolished by Cubbitt's grandson as it was too expensive to restore and maintain. The estate was sold in 1984, and the first vines were planted soon afterwards. The estate lies on the west side, under Ranmore Common and on the north side of Dorking. It is one of the first of the new English vineyards and now the largest by some margin, producing quite a range of vintages, some of which have won major awards. In fact, grapes were grown in this area in Roman times, but the climate has varied over the centuries such that vines were unknown in the Downs for many hundreds of years. The climate is now warmer, and the south east facing slopes on which Denbies lies get a lot of sun, allowing the vines to thrive. The chalk that comprises the North Downs is the same geological formation as that underlying the Champagne region in France, and these days English sparkling and still wines are among the best in the World.

Left: Looking north up the lines of vines to Denbies winery and visitor centre, which plays host to many thousands of people each year, and behind with Norbury Park and its house in the background

Right: Ripe grapes still on the vines with Box Hill behind: the green field on the right leads up to the grassy picnic area where people picnic and enjoy the view

The Mole Gap: Mickleham and the Stepping Stones

On the journey from its source in East Sussex to its confluence with the Thames at East Molesley, the River Mole passes Dorking and, where it meets the Downs, has carved a steep cliff in the west side of Box Hill at the Mole Gap. Chalk is relatively soft rock and, being calcium carbonate, is soluble in water and prone to being eroded rapidly by river currents. Thus the river has also eroded its bedrock to form sinkholes and underground caves into which water can completely disappear from the surface during very dry periods, whilst the river continues to run underground.

Although there have been pollution incidents in the past, these days the water quality is very good and the river contains many different fish species, including chub, dace, barbel, brown trout, perch and pike, some of which are marker species for good water quality. The area contains a number of Sites of Special Scientific Interest (SSSI) and attracts a lot of local and visitor interest in its conservation. Maintaining a good ecology is not easy as the Mole Gap is a busy place, with the well-used A24 running through it, a railway line, two villages, farms, and many, many visitors.

The Mole Stepping Stones

There are a number of footbridges that cross the river, including one on the Pilgrim's Way, at the bottom of the precipitous descent from Box Hill. This was not always the case, and it used to be necessary to ford the river a little up-stream where the stream is relatively wide and shallow except when in flood. This was inconvenient at best, so stepping stones were placed there to avoid getting one's feet wet. These were made permanent in 1946, when the current concrete stones were installed, but they still don't solve the problem when the river is high and covers them completely. Nowadays, the nearby footbridge offers a safe crossing at all times.

Mickleham

This is one of the Box Hill villages, situated on the lower slopes of the hill on the east bank of the river. It ranges steeply up the hillside and along the main road and boasts two good pubs, a restaurant and two schools as well as its church and the Juniper Hall Field Centre. There has been a church in this location since Saxon times, and much of St Michael's Church, pictured on the left, is Norman.

The zig-zag road up Box Hill starts here, passing the church and the Running Horse pub within Mickleham before climbing up the grassy hill to the summit. This has been a particularly popular challenge for cyclists following its inclusion the London 2012 Olympics cycle events.

Left: St Michael and All Angels Church, Mickleham
Right: The Stepping Stones across the River Mole

Ranmore Common

Ranmore Common spreads across the down to the north west of Dorking and is almost all covered in a mature and dense woodland that runs nearly continuously along the ridge for eight miles to Guildford. The North Downs and Pilgrim's Ways run through the common, along the ridge top, and there are many footpaths criss-crossing it that are well used by walkers and horse riders. The hamlet of Ranmore is comprised of a few houses and St Barnabas' Church, which was built by Sir George Cubitt of Denbies in 1859, but almost all the Ranmore land is managed by the National Trust for recreational access.

There are lovely views across the Vale Of Holmesdale over Wotton and back to Dorking from the open grassland of the southern ridge, but when you enter the forest, it is a different world. Huge beech, oak and ash trees rise up from the deep leaf-litter floor, from which spring a great number and variety of fungi each autumn, and between them holly and other shrubs can make the forest very dense. Most of the main tracks run northwards, descending into the valley below Polesden Lacey, and they can be very wet and muddy after rain. The forest ends at the fields of Yewtree Farm, and on one of its borders lies the famous Tanners Hatch Youth Hostel which has no vehicular access, making it an excellent rural retreat.

Left: Walkers ascending from Yewtree Farm on a footpath across the Polesden Lacey Estate, with Ranmore Common behind

Right: A view south across Holmesdale from the Pilgrim's Way on the Ranmore ridge

Chalk, Greensand and Fungi

Ranmore Common (right) lies on the ridge of Downs chalk that we have been following since Dover, but the chalk ends at the base of the scarp slope and the underlying rock becomes greensand. South and west of Dorking, this forms hills that have a different character from the chalk downs, as the acidity and drainage qualities promote very different soils and vegetation. Chalky soil is neutral or slightly alkaline and porous, whilst sandstone is impermeable and water collects on it and tends to become acidic from vegetation decay. In such places this slow decomposition of vegetable matter forms peat over long periods of time.

Mushrooms and Toadstools

These hills are very rich in fungi of all sorts, and the variety in ancient woods such as these is astonishing: the entire soil is laced with fungal hyphae that produce strange and colourful fruiting bodies, or mushrooms. These hyphae also merge into the roots of trees, becoming known as 'mycorrhiza' forming a symbiotic relationship that the trees depend upon for their healthy existence, especially where the soil is nutrient-poor.

The red and white Fly Agaric (*Amanita muscari*) is very characteristic of Leith Hill, and has a confusing name as it is actually one of the *Amanita* genus, whereas agarics are the sort of mushrooms you find in your local supermarket. Most *Amanitas* are poisonous (e.g. the 'death cap'), and whilst the fly agaric isn't known to be deadly, it contains a neurotoxin that results in unpredictable hallucinations for the eater that can be very unpleasant.

Shaggy ink caps (top right) are edible when young, and pop up in surprising clumps on disturbed soil: those pictured were in a field below the Downs near Westcott.

In Ranmore you can find many edible mushrooms, such as the bay boletus, hedgehog mushrooms, and even chanterelles (lower right). There are also oddities like the upright coral (lower left), and a number of poisonous ones that may be easily confused with edible varieties; even the experts get fooled at times!

Left:
Upper left: Fly Agaric (*Amanita muscari*)
Upper right: Shaggy Ink Caps (*Coprinus comatus*)
Lower left: Upright coral (*Ramaria stricta*)
Lower right: Chanterelles (*Cantharellus cibarius*)

Right: A ride through Ranmore Common

At Polesden Lacey

Polesden Lacey is a historic house and estate on a ridge just north of Ranmore Common, separated from it by a farmed valley. There has been a house in this position since the 14th century, but it has been demolished and rebuilt more than once. The current house was started in 1824 and extended in 1906 and was the location of many society receptions and events held by its owners, Ronald and Margaret Greville. The most famous visitors were the Duke and Duchess of York (later King George VI and Queen Elizabeth) who, in 1923, spent their honeymoon there.

Mrs Greville left the house to the National Trust in 1942, for whom it is one of their most popular destinations with nearly 300,000 visitors a year. As well as visiting the House which is very grand and full of period treasures, there are extensive gardens that are well maintained and developed by the Trust. The walled kitchen garden pictured to the right was transformed in Mrs Greville's time into a rose garden, and the early 20th-century style is maintained with softly pastel coloured roses.

Left: The drive and east wing of Polesden Lacey House with Ranmore Common in the background

Below: Snowdrops in the gardens

Right: View through one of the round holes in the wall of the rose garden

Leith Hill Tower

Walking south from Ranmore Common you pass through a series of very different landscapes within a short distance: initial deep woods become chalk grassland descending into the valley, where the fertile land is intensively farmed and dotted with settlements, including Westcott and Wotton. As you start to climb the south side of the valley, the woods are a bit more open, mostly oak, birch and ash, and you start to see more bracken in clearings. You are on the slopes of Leith Hill, the tallest hill in Surrey at 294 metres.

On the higher slopes, the forest is mostly birch and pine with bracken covering the ground, and the open areas are a rough stony heath, covered in bracken and bilberry. You will also notice that the path you walk upon is sandy rather than smooth and whitish: it is a very different vegetation from the Downs.

The peak of Leith Hill is surmounted by the 18th-century tower that was built to raise the hill's height above 1,000 feet (305 metres). It was built as a residence originally but having been closed for a lengthy period, has been restored by the National Trust and is now open to the public to climb and enjoy the view.

The Hill is the first of a small range running west to meet the River Wey which mostly wooded, apart from a few small farms and hamlets. The village of Coldharbour is below the summit, strewn along the road from Dorking, with its lovely old Plough Inn. The village also boasts a cricket club with its pitch and pavilion perched on a piece of level ground a hundred feet or so higher up the hill. It is a very pretty place with lovely views, and the site is also used for the annual Guy Fawkes party with a big bonfire that is visible for many miles.

To the south of the summit is Leith Hill Place, a palladian mansion that was owned by the composer, Ralph Vaughan Williams until he died and left it to the National Trust, so it is open to the public.

Left: The sandy Surrey Heath landscape of pines, birch and bilberry on the slopes of Leith Hill

Right: The east side of Leith Hill Tower on a sunny Sunday morning where off-road cyclists and walkers queue at the National Trust snack bar

Leith Hill Villages

Friday Street is a hamlet tucked away in the woods, a favourite beauty spot which is a lovely surprise when stumbled upon during a walk or car ride. It includes a few houses spread up a cul-de-sac, the Stephen Langton Inn, and Hammer Pond with its accompanying mill house. It is a very peaceful place, though it might not have been if developers in the 1930s had had their way, as it was advertised for sale as 'a choice freehold building estate, absolutely unrestricted'. Fortunately it was saved by £3,000 of public donations.

A similar subscription saved Abinger Common (below left) which is a mile or so to the west. The image is taken from its 11th-century St James Church and you can see part of the Abinger Hatch pub behind. This is part of the Parish of Abinger which spreads over rather a large area, covering this village along with Sutton Abinger and its Volunteer pub (right), Abinger Hammer, Forest Green, Walliswood, Oakwood Hill and some outskirts of Holmbury St Mary. The fact that the area is so sparsely populated means that it remains full of charm and beauty.

Left: Hammer Pond at Friday Street
Below: St James's Churchyard at Abinger Common
Right: The Volunteer Inn at Sutton Abinger

Wotton and the Tilling Valley

Friday Street is on a stream that feeds into Tilling Bourne (also known as the River Tillingbourne) which runs steeply down from here through the park land of Wotton House, where it veers west towards Guildford to join the River Wey. Its valley, which is part of Holmesdale, is known as the Tilling Valley and contains the pretty villages of Abinger Hammer, Shere and Albury.

John Evelyn, the diarist was born at Wotton House in 1620 and subsequently inherited it. At that time, a substantial part of the area had been stripped of trees and had lost its charm, so he devoted much his life to tree planting and landscaping the entire estate, the results of which we benefit from today.

Wotton House is now a hotel and conference centre with over 100 bedrooms.

The hamlet of Wotton lies a few yards further south, by the main Dorking-Guildford road across which sits St John's Church on its own spur, with a magnificent view in all directions.

Overleaf Left: St John's Church, Wotton
Overleaf Right: The Tillingbourne Valley lies directly underneath Hackhust and Blatchford Downs, which are owned and managed by the National Trust

Rhododendrons: Beauty and the Beast

The image on the left shows rhododendrons forming huge bushes and covering the floor of a wood north of Wotton, but it could be many places throughout Britain and Ireland. The shrub is *Rhododendron ponticum*, a native of southern Europe which has been introduced as a decorative shrub. It grows fast, producing large bushes that produce huge numbers of seeds and also reproduces by suckering, covering acid soils rapidly. In addition, it excludes other species by shutting out light and also by coating the soil with a fibrous root system.

In Surrey, the problem is not yet too bad and where it starts to take over, as here, it will be fairly accessible and relatively easily controlled. This is in contrast to parts of Wales and Ireland where it has taken over entire mountain sides and forests.

Some Rhododendron species are far less invasive and dangerous, and deciduous azaleas such as the golden specimen on the right bring colour and a gorgeous scent to a garden.

Far Left: *Rhododendron pontecum* in the Tilling Valley
Left: A *Rhododendron pontecum* flower
Above: A golden Azalea in a Surrey Hills garden

The 'Stop Line' and Pillboxes

As you walk along the Pilgrim's Way through Surrey, especially along the top of the ridge between Westcott and Farnham, you come across brick and concrete pillboxes quite often. These are what remain of a line of World War II defences that were part of the GHQ Stop Line that dotted our landscape from Kent to Somerset, and from the Thames estuary to The Wash. The pillboxes here are within the section that runs from Westcott to north of Farnham.

Following Dunkirk, the military planners installed many layers of defence designed to hold up any German advance based upon predicted landing points and routes, of which lines of pill boxes were one component. The example on the left is a 'type 24' pillbox, which is an irregular hexagon with a flat top on which a tower or equipment could be placed. It still has an open view into the distance, and at the time, this would have been the case for all of them. However many have been covered by trees and other vegetation, as in the 'type 22' version to the right, or destroyed. They are now listed as historical monuments and more care is taken of them.

Of course, in society's eyes, the defence of the realm is always the first priority, so the protection of ancient woods and wonderful landscape could be seen as a 'nice to have' that will always be sacrificed on the altar of war. Therefore it is, perhaps, ironic that these ugly structures should now be protected, having been imposed upon a previously green landscape. However pillboxes are part of our history, and it is human action over the centuries that has fashioned much of this landscape.

Left: A 'type 24' pillbox on the chalk grassland above Abinger Hammer
Right: An overgrown, decrepit pillbox near Farnham

Overleaf Left: Autumn woodland path near Abinger
Overleaf right: Cyclists descend the Downs on a steep lane towards Abinger

Abinger Hammer

This is the first of a series of pretty villages that lie on the banks of Tilling Bourne on its way west towards the River Wey. The village's main claim to fame is the clock which overhangs a bend in the main road and has a little statue of "Jack the Blacksmith", who strikes the hour with his hammer. It dates from the early 20th century and was commissioned and paid for by the villagers, with a large donation by Sir Thomas Farrer, a retired senior civil servant. It commemorates the fact that between the 17th and 19th centuries an iron industry supported people in the Tillingbourne Valley. The hammer-ponds that supplied the water to the forges are still to be seen today along the course of the River.

The A25 from Dorking passes through the village with views of the river as it runs through a charming green where families picnic and children play. At the eastern end of the green you will often see veteran sports cars waiting to be serviced by the specialist Abinger Hammer Motors.

Left: The Abinger Hammer clock and Jack The Blacksmith

Right: Vintage sports cars at Abinger Hammer Motors

Overleaf Left: Looking east along Holmesdale from near Wotton church, with Dorking town in the middle and the southern scarp of the Downs on the left.

Overleaf Right: Many of the country lanes that wind through the Surrey Hills are 'sunken' or 'hollow' lanes, particularly where the underlying rock is greensand. They have usually become that way through hundreds of years of traffic passing over the sandstone and loosening sand from it, which is then washed away by rain. They can be very deep and sometimes huge tree roots become exposed and can look quite spectacular.

In the days when these roads were unpaved, they were steep, rutted, slippery and dangerous, and very difficult to negotiate with a loaded cart. In fact, even in the 19th century, this area of Surrey was thought of as remote and rather wild, particularly as so much of the land was thickly forested.

Shere Village

Snug in its valley on the Tillingbourne below the downs and surrounded by picturesque farms, cottages and settlements, the beauty and charm of Shere has been widely known for a long time. Its roads wind sinuously between its many old and lovely buildings, and it has been spared the heavy traffic of the A25 since a bypass was built. On a sunny weekend, it can still get rather congested with cars carrying visitors who want to enjoy the rural peace and charm, but the village and its surrounds have been loved and protected from inappropriate development because it is valued by residents, visitors and many artists.

The White Horse pub has been serving ale through the centuries, and its outlook over a little green with the church behind it has hardly altered, apart from the roads becoming paved. The visitor can sit outside the pub on a nice day and watch life pass by down Middle Street, or wander down to the Tillingbourne and watch the ducks dabble in the dappled shade.

It wasn't always thus, as in the 17th century there were twenty mills doing weaving and tanning along the twelve mile length of the Tillingbourne and four of these were in the parish. Mill wheel of Gomshall Mill is still attached to building, which is a restaurant now. There were local sheep to provide the wool which was spun by the women before weaving and clean water from the hard working little river.

The concept of the English rural idyll, with its old cottages, copses and streams has been fostered by many artists, to the extent that, according to Peter Brandon in his book on the North Downs, "By the 1890s landscape artists were descending on west Surrey in clouds.... and multiplying artists' colonies were turning the south-east into a vast open-air studio...", and creating an entire school of English painting. One who is still known is George Marks, who lived in Shere and painted the local countryside.

Left: The White Horse pub
Right: The Middle Street, Shere with Netley Down rising in the background

St James Church, Shere

A History of the County of Surrey calls St James church 'second to none in Surrey for beauty and antiquarian interest'. It sits opposite the pub and is shown here with the much more recent war memorial. The lychgate was designed by Edwin Lutyens, one of the foremost architects in Edwardian England and he also designed some cottages in Shere for the Bray family, hereditary Lords of the Manor. The church dates from 1190 and probably replaced a wooden Saxon church. The walls of the church are built from a fascinating jumble of materials, from re-used Roman tiles to clunch, flint, Caen stone imported from Normandy, Tudor bricks, and local stone.

Left: An old cottage in Shere
Below: River Tillingbourne in the middle of the village
Right: St James Church and the war memorial

Albury: a moving village

The Church of St Peter and St Paul in Albury Park (left) is known locally as 'The Saxon Church' to distinguish it from the parish church in the village of Albury itself. Albury Park is a private estate in a lovely position on the banks of the Tillingbourne, but once was the location of Albury village. However, an 18th-century landowner, Captain Finch, wanted to establish a park around his house and he started a tortuous (and often unpleasant) process of having the village moved a mile to the west to its present location! The main road from Shere was blocked, and a new one constructed to the village, and then the old church was left on its own in the park, though it continued to be used as the Parish Church until 1842.

At this time, Henry Drummond owned the manor and used his wealth (he was a banker) to build himself a new mansion, but also to have the new church of St Peter and St Paul built in an elevated position in the village, along with a number of fine houses. The Saxon Church was then closed and fell into disrepair. These days, the church is maintained by the Churches Conservation Trust and by the Friends of Albury Old Church, who had a new roof put on it after it had been open to the air for a hundred years. It is now open for visitors and occasionally used for services.

Within the parish, there is also has a rather grand Catholic apostolic church between the two on the Sherbourne brook and the small 'Barn Church' of St Michael just up the road at Farley Green.

Silent Pool

Silent Pool is a small spring-fed lake just above Albury and within the Albury Estate in a very romantic setting. There are few lakes in the Downs, and though small, this is a very pretty spot at the foot of the Downs. It is surrounded by trees which absorb sound and whose reflections lend it an air of mystery and contemplation that has provoked legends. The pool feeds directly into Sherbourne Pond which is within a farm of the same name, and Sherbourne Brook runs the short distance down the hill to join the River Tillingbourne close to Albury.

The field immediately to the west of the Pool, on the Downs slope, is now a vineyard that produces a wine called Silent Pool Rose.

Left: The 'Saxon Church' in Albury Park
Right: Silent Pool

The Chimneys of Albury

Henry Drummond, the owner of Albury Park who built the new church, also built a number of houses in and around the displaced village. He seems to have had a penchant for substantial Elizabethan-style chimneys because these have been placed upon the mansion he built within his Park and also on several village buildings: that on the left was originally a row of shops. The ground floor is faced with brick and stones set in mortar, the first floor is overhanging and tiled, which is a style common throughout Surrey, and there is a lot of detail in the carved woodwork. It seems, therefore, that Drummond was not concerned with cost, but was interested in the architecture and detail of the many buildings he commissioned.

Albury Downs and Newlands Corner

If you walk along the main road in a westerly direction through Albury, cross the Tillingbourne and then go straight on where the road bends sharply to the left, you climb steeply up 300 feet to the top of Albury Downs. This is a famous beauty spot, where you will also encounter the A25 at Newlands Corner (you get here quicker by car, but miss a lot). Here there is a car park, a cafe and a visitor centre, and you are on the Pilgrim's Way once more, from which you get yet another gorgeous view south, across the woods and fields of Tillingbourne Valley to the sandstone hills.

The visitor centre and open areas are managed by the Surrey Wildlife Trust who are custodians of some of the most important landscapes in Surrey. They work to protect and regenerate Surrey's wildlife and inform the public and provide opportunities to experience the landscape and wildlife at their best – http://www.surreywildlifetrust.org/

St Martha's Church

If you follow the Pilgrim's Way from Albury Downs, which are chalk, in about a kilometre you come to a road where the Way turns left, down the hill to a T junction. At this point, the Way leaves the road, heading uphill, and you are now on greensand, and the path at your feet is sandy. When you emerge from the woods at the top of the hill, St Martha's Church is in front of you and you are in a churchyard with fabulous views all around. This building was constructed in the 19th century, with medieval features, as the previous church had fallen into ruin. There was a church here in medieval times, and the hill also has the remains of megalithic structures dating from as far back as the Neolithic.

Left: An Albury House with ornate chimneys from Henry Drummond's time
Right: The view from Albury Downs
Overleaf: St Martha's Church and churchyard

Chantries and Pewley Down

Continuing west on the Pilgrim's Way from St Martha's the path descends, then skirts the north side of the Chantries which, along with Pewley Down, is part of a swathe of land bought by Guildford Borough Council in 1936. The intention was to prevent house building, which had started on the north side of Pewley Down from creeping south, smothering the lovely countryside in concrete. In this it has succeeded famously, although there is always pressure to develop, and the temptation of the money that the Council could earn. As it is, the entire area is hugely popular with local residents for walking, cycling and horse riding. Emerging from the suburbia of Longdown Road onto the wide open grassy slopes is always a lovely contrast and surprise.

Chantries is a tree-covered hill that was a sheep pasture at one time, but has been planted with a mixture of commercial conifers and mixed deciduous woodland, including some coppices. Parts of it have been felled and replaced over the years, but the fact that it has been more carefully managed in recent times has resulted in the recovery of ancient woodland flowers, including bluebells and wood anemones (see the left image foreground). Commercial forest still covers some areas, but if the plan is to replace this with a more natural, mixed woodland, it has to be very carefully managed to protect indigenous species and promote biodiversity.

Pewley Down is a good example of creeping urbanisation, with streets reaching up the hill, like tentacles. One such street has taken up the crest of the Down, in order to put larger houses in the best position. Below this, the Down is open and breezy with magnificent views, and seems quite large when you are on it, but a glance at an Ordnance Survey map shows that it wouldn't have taken long for it to become submerged in concrete.

It is now a Local Nature Reserve, and the Natural England web site listing says:

> "Pewley Down is chalk grassland, renowned for its unusual flowers, and the butterflies which depend on these. On Pewley Down 26 species of butterfly were recorded in 2010, and 119 species of bees, wasps and ants. There are also rare flowers, including 6 species of orchid."

Left: The footpath from Chantries, with wood anemones
Right: Pewley Down

Guildford

Guildford spreads out across the Downs on either side of the River Wey, starting where the river cuts through its gap between Pewley Down and the most westerly finger of the North Downs ridge, known as the Hog's Back.

The town has Saxon origins, and its name derives from 'gelde', meaning gold, rather than 'guild'. As well as being a place to ford the river, the location would have benefited from being on an old route called the Harrow Way as well as on the Pilgrim's Way. The castle is Norman, built where it guards the Wey gap and all other routes through it, and although it has not been involved in any recorded conflict, it has been visited by some medieval kings and queens. These days, the castle grounds have been turned into a public park and the keep is open to the public.

The River Wey is of variable depth and width and has many bends, so was not an efficient means of transport. This problem was addressed when the Wey Navigation canal was completed between Guildford and the Thames at Weybridge in 1653, an event which gave a great boost to Guildford's commerce and it can now be seen running alongside the river. In the 19th century, the Wey Navigation was extended and joined to other waterways that gave people access to the entire south of England by water.

These days, Guildford is the county town of Surrey with a university, a cathedral and a thriving commercial life. The need for water transport has gone, of course, as road and rail links have improved such that it can take under an hour to get to and from the centre of London, so is another good location for commuters. Nowadays the waterways are well used for rowing, boating, picnics and walks, the River Wey providing particularly lovely scenery as it meanders south to Shalford and beyond.

Left: The River Wey at the gap in the Downs
Right: Guildford Castle

The aerial photograph is looking south over the cathedral and University of Surrey. Behind the cathedral, in the shade, is the southern edge of Guildford which rises up the slopes of the Hog's Back. To the right, the dual carriageway is the A3 London to Portsmouth road, which climbs up to the top of the ridge where the A31 splits off, traversing the entire crest to Farnham.

Hopefully these days it wouldn't be possible to build a major road in such a damaging place, but the Hog's Back is under further threat. At the time of writing, the farmland in the image above along with an ancient wood that borders recently developed land are under threat from a major housing development application by the University. If this is allowed, roads and houses would cover this pretty, productive land and severely endanger the rich natural history of the woods and hedgerows. It would be the sort of urban sprawl that the Green Belt legislation was supposed to prevent, as Guildford suburbs creep towards Farnham.

Whilst population is growing, more housing is needed, but it should surely be located to make the most efficient use of land rather than destroying the Green Belt for financial gain! A campaign launched to prevent this development recalls the grass-roots campaigns of the last century in places like Banstead Commons, and it seems that the battle to conserve the Downs landscape will be unending whilst the pressures grow.

Left: Aerial photograph of Guildford Cathedral and the University of Surrey. **Above:** The view south from the slopes of the Hog's Back at Blackwell Farm

Mother Ludlum's Cave

This small cave has been naturally hollowed out of the sandstone by a spring of clear water. It is to be found by the Greensand Way footpath just south of Farnham, on the banks of the River Wey and within the Moor Park Nature Reserve. It was valued as a good water supply by the monks of Waverley Abbey (page 96) and became known as St Mary's Well, and there were once iron cups on chains for passers-by to drink from.

Mother Ludlum was supposed to have been a white witch who lived in the cave, but there are several legends linking the cave, the witch and a cauldron that resides in Frensham church nearby. One version of the legend describes how the devil asked to borrow the witch's cauldron, and when she refused, he ran away with it, his hoof prints creating some hills near Churt, known as the Devil's Jumps.

The cave area was renovated and turned into a small grotto in the 19th century and the ironstone entrance arch added. It is now of great interest because it provides a roost for several bat species: Natterer's Bat (*Myotis nattereri*), Daubenton's Bat (*M. daubentonii*) and Long-eared Bat (*Plecotus auritus*), for whose protection the ornamental gate has been added.

In the image below of the interior, you can see where the cave has been naturally hollowed out by water, and where it has been artificially opened out in the foreground. Sadly, the golden pile is dead leaves, rather than gold leaf!

A Path up Crooksbury Hill, South of Farnham

This is part of Crooksbury and Puttenham Common, which is a large area of forest and heath south of the Hog's Back. Like a lot of Surrey heaths, most of the open areas are now covered by scrub or planted forest leaving limited heather-covered open areas, which are now protected as SSSIs.

The path heads up to the top of Crooksbury Hill, which is the highest hill in the common, and the silver birch and pine are typical of forests that grow on these acidic soils. The ground is covered by bracken which in many places becomes a pest in the summer, sometimes growing to head height and covering any spare ground. It is inedible to livestock and spreads quickly through underground rhizomes. Two Bronze Age hoards have been discovered on Crooksbury Hill.

Overleaf Left: Remains of Waverley Abbey
Founded in 1128, Waverley Abbey was Britain's first Cistercian monastery; in its heyday it covered 60 acres and was lived in by nearly two hundred monks and lay brothers, although it was not wealthy. It was closed and the monks dispersed in the Dissolution under Henry VIII in 1536 and the land was given to Sir William FitzWilliam. In the 18th century, a new mansion was built on the north side of the estate, partly using stones from the Abbey buildings, remains of which were left as a decaying landscape feature.

Overleaf Right: The Lake at Waverley

Farnham

At Farnham, we reach the end of our journey along the North Downs. We have travelled 100 miles as the crow flies from Dover, crossing the width of Kent and Surrey, and ending with the thin spine of the Hog's Back. The North Downs Way long distance footpath starts (or ends) at Farnham, as does the Pilgrim's Way, though it used to continue as far as Winchester.

The town is on the northern branch of the River Wey and has evolved from settlements going back up to 7,000 years into prehistory. Taking into account the prevalence of bracken in the area, it is not surprising that its name derives from the Saxon 'Fearnhamme', where the word 'fearn' means fern. The manor containing Farnham was owned by the Bishop of Winchester from the 7th century AD right through to the mid 20th century.

Farnham has been a successful market town since at least the 18th century and still acts as a local commercial centre. Its main industry from Roman times was pottery, using the local clay, and the 'Greenware' of the Farnham Pottery became well known during the 19th and 20th centuries, attracting the interest of the Arts and Crafts Movement. The town has become something of a centre for the Arts, and hosts a campus of The University of the Creative Arts, which evolved from the Farnham School of Art as well as having a craft study centre. There is also The Maltings creative arts centre which is very active in all the fine arts, and the New Ashgate Gallery of contemporary art.

Farnham retains many fine buildings whose architecture reflects styles throughout the ages and a stroll through the older streets is a real walk through history, culminating in the fascinating and important castle and bishop's palace.

Left: Church Lane in central Farnham leading to St Andrew's Church
Right: The interior of The Nelson Arms pub in Castle Street

Farnham castle

Farnham lies on several ancient routes, including the Pilgrim's Way and the Harrow Way and is half way between Winchester and London. This would have been a two day journey by horse, and everyone would have passed through Farnham at the end of day one, making it a convenient place to rest. The Bishops of Winchester were very rich and powerful and, in the 12th century, close to the Norman kings. They would have frequently made the journey to and from London so were provided with the castle by King Stephen's brother, Henry de Blois.

The Norman castle remained important until the Civil Wars, when the castle was fought over, changing hands between the Parliamentarians and Royalists several times until in 1648 Oliver Cromwell had the keep partially dismantled to make it defenceless. Subsequently, King Charles I stayed overnight in West Street on his way to London for his trial and subsequent execution.

The bishop's palace has developed since the 12th century and includes fine buildings from various subsequent periods. It remained in the ownership of the Bishopric of Winchester until 1927, when it became the residence of the Bishop of Guildford. This ceased in 1955 and it is now an international conference centre, with public access to the castle keep and parts of the bishop's palace.

Left: The front of the bishop's palace
Right: The main gate into the castle remains

Conclusion

So our journey across the North Downs ends at Farnham, as it began, with ancient ramparts put up in defence of the Realm. As we have seen, the entire length of the North Downs presents a line of defence with its steep scarp, penetrated by a few rivers which are mostly defended by stone castles, or brick pillboxes. Hand in hand with the military theme has been the Pilgrim's Way, upon which pilgrims, bishops and merchants, saints and sinners have travelled for thousands of years to and from England's prime gateway at Dover.

We have traced the geology, the landscape and the ancient Ways, finding snippets of history that often illuminate how the present scenery came about. We have learned a little about the diverse natural history of the Downs and its unique and fragile ecologies which support rare and beautiful flora and fauna, and how we simultaneously protect and threaten their survival.

As well as being a rich farming area, the beauty of these chalk hills attracts people seeking to enjoy the scenery and fresh air, but is also a very tempting prospect for property developers to make serious money out of putting open land under concrete, or golf courses. So nowadays, the battle is to defend the natural beauty and diversity of the Downs, to prevent a gorgeous countryside, rich in species like those that grace this page, from becoming smothered in uniform suburbia and roads. In this fight, it is not castles and walls that are of value, but the people who live there banding together, determined to stop the urban sprawl. Bodies like the National Trust, The Woodland Trust, the Wildlife Trusts and the RSPB continue to work to save and restore the landscape, but it is you and I who will decide whether that unending fight will succeed.

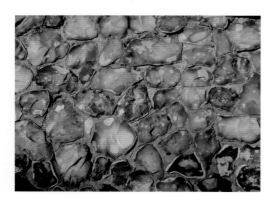

Images on this page, anti-clockwise from the top left:
Spindle seeds in autumn on Hackhurst Downs; species-rich meadow on the Downs ridge in West Kent; The flint-dressed wall of St Mary's Church at Headley; a bumble bee feeding on a thistle on White Downs; a Meadow Brown butterfly on wild thyme flowers near Dover; ripe grapes at Denbies Winery; bluebells in Margery Wood; a Brimstone butterfly on hawks-beard at lower Bush in Kent.

References and Indexes

Acknowledgements

In writing the text for this book, I gained a lot of background and some detail from Peter Brandon's book entitled *The North Downs* (Phillimore & Co. Ltd., 2005). I accessed a great deal of information through Google, and often used Wikipedia as a starting point for a particular location. I also accessed many local web sites, and information about listed buildings through the English Heritage website, and about areas with statutory environmental protection as SSSIs through English Nature's website. Some information on long distance walking routes was collected from the National Trails website.

I am very grateful to my friend Andrew Sherratt who took me up in a little Cessna airplane to take aerial photographs across the length of the North Downs.

Also, thanks to Tom Stevens of the Hog's Back campaign for the image on page 93.

I also collected pamphlets and magazines for local information as I came across them in my travels.

Conservation Organisations

The National Trust
www.nationaltrust.org.uk
0344 800 1895

The Woodland Trust
www.woodlandtrust.org.uk
01476 581137

Wildlife Trusts
http://www.wildlifetrusts.org/
01636 677711

English Heritage
www.english-heritage.org.uk
0870 333 1181

Natural England
www.naturalengland.org.uk

North Downs Way
http://www.nationaltrail.co.uk/north-downs-way

Index of Place Names

This is an index of places and rivers mentioned or shown in the book.

Index of images and map references